NQT SU͟͟͟͟ GUIDE

Emily Webb and Matthew Farn

NQT SURVIVAL GUIDE

Emily Webb and Matthew Farn

A division of MA Education Ltd

Teach Books Division, MA Education Ltd, St Jude's Church,
Dulwich Road, London SE24 0PB

British Library Cataloguing-in-Publication Data
A catalogue record is available for this book

© MA Education Limited 2006
ISBN-10 1 85642 343 3
ISBN-13 978 1 85642 343 4

Printed by Athenaeum Press Ltd, Dukesway, Team Valley,
Gateshead, NE11 0PZ

CONTENTS

INTRODUCTION

There are any number of helpful hints and tips in this book, and you will want to try most of them at some point in your first year. However, in order to preserve your sanity, it is really important not to try all of them at once.

Teaching is about making the best of your time so that you are the most effective teacher you can be. You have to be able to work smart as well as hard.

The best advice anyone can give you is to be prepared. Plan your lessons using your staff planner; write a few lines that will help you to run your lessons effectively.

Try not dwell on a bad experience, but do learn from it. Make a mental note of what didn't work and try another strategy; talk to your colleagues, see what works for them and try to adapt it to work for you. Other teachers will provide you with the greatest source of support, so be sure to use that network of support to the full. No one will think less of you if you ask for help and most people are pleased to be asked for their advice.

There is no such thing as "just a teacher". So when you hear the expression "those who can, do; those who can't, teach" or when friends start ribbing you about the easy life you lead because you finish work at 3.30pm and have more holidays than they do, just remember that you possess the following skills and must put them into practice every minute of your working day:

- planning and organisational skills
- communication and presentation skills
- problem solving
- determination, commitment and initiative
- flexibility and adaptability
- the ability to motivate others
- enthusiasm and passion

- leadership and teamwork
- creativity
- assertiveness
- patience and understanding.

Most people can only dream of listing those skills on their CV, whereas you will be using all of them in your first year of teaching and beyond.

After the nerve-wracking day-long interview and the observed lesson with the class from hell, you face the panel of senior staff and the personal interview, questions coming at you thick and fast. The question "Are you still interested in this post?" is repeated over the course of the day. What is it all for? That wonderful moment when the position is offered to you.

That's when your adventures really begin.

Some people may think that teachers are born into the profession, but most are made over a period of time that starts when you first stand in front of a class of expectant faces. If your experience is anything like most, then you will have started with the "easy" year seven classes and worked your way up to the far more challenging key stage 4. Normally, during your training, you will have had the opportunity to team-teach these more advanced groups. Now, you are going to be expected to manage on your own.

There are so many different things you are going to need to know in order to provide the students in front of you with a balanced and full educational experience. This guide aims to cover some of the most important aspects that we feel you may need to know during your first year in the educational system: what was once called "the probation year" and is now better known as the "Newly Qualified Teacher year". At the end of your NQT year, if you pass a series of observations (plus the English, Maths and ICT online tests – the bane of many an NQT's existence) you will receive your Department for Education and Science (DfES) number and will achieve Qualified Teacher Status (QTS). This means that the government will recognise your full qualifications as a state school trained teacher.

The role of teacher has changed significantly over the past few years, as has the training. This has become much more rigorous, as you well know, having just completed your chosen route through teacher training. Teachers today have a much wider role to fulfil than they have ever had. Gone are the days when you simply delivered a lesson to thirty students and forgot about them. The intricacies of the modern education system call for far more careful planning, preparation and accountability. Some critics feel that teachers today train their pupils to pass exams and are not really teaching them anything that they may use after they leave the compulsory education system. Others feel that education has moved beyond mere exams and is aiming to teach in a holistic environment. We will discuss the various theories in a later chapter.

This book aims to provide you with useful information that will prepare you for the exciting and ever-developing world of education in which you have chosen to make your career.

After the initial euphoria of getting your first teaching post, the cold light of day dawns. In September you will set out on a career that may last in excess of thirty years (although the national average for recent NQTs remaining in teaching is a very depressing three years).

You should remember that there will always be a need for good teachers and if you have a real interest in your new career, then it will keep you busy until you retire. Schools may change, governments may change, the requirements of the National Curriculum will certainly change, but the essential job of educating students will never change. The whole reason they come to you is to learn from your experiences.

YOUR INDUCTION YEAR

THE PURPOSE

The DfES introduced a compulsory period of induction for NQTs in September 1999. The induction period must be undertaken by NQTs who wish to work in maintained schools and non-maintained special schools. The induction period may also be taken while working in city technology colleges, independent schools and, since September 2000, in sixth form colleges. It will also be possible to undertake induction while working in city academies. During the induction period you have to show that you continue to meet the standards of QTS, and meet all the induction standards.

You should have an individualised programme of support during your induction year from a designated induction tutor. This includes observation of your teaching, opportunities to watch more experienced teachers both in and outside your school, and a professional review of progress at least every half-term.

It is the responsibility of the headteacher to ensure that you do not teach more than ninety per cent of a normal timetable during your induction period, to allow your induction to take place. This generally means that you will get one extra non-teaching period. A further minimum ten per cent of an NQT's reduced timetable must be assigned as guaranteed planning, preparation and assessment time.

The headteacher is responsible with appropriate bodies (for maintained schools and non-maintained special schools this is the local education authority (LEA), and for independent schools, it is either any LEA in England or a special body, the Independent Schools' Council Teacher Induction Panel) and will make a final recommendation as to whether a new teacher has passed or failed. The appropriate body makes the final decision, and there is a right of appeal to the General Teaching Council for England (GTCE).

THE ROLE OF YOUR INDUCTION TUTOR

Your induction tutor should be an experienced teacher who has close contact with you, for example your line manager or a senior member of staff. If there is no member of staff who is available or who has the relevant experience to fulfil this role, the headteacher may be your induction tutor. Under the regulations, there is a clear responsibility placed on schools to provide NQTs with support from an induction tutor.

The induction tutor's role is:

- To provide day-to-day monitoring and support. If the support function is allocated to another teacher, this should be clearly specified at the beginning of induction.
- To undertake most of the observations of your teaching and provide constructive feedback.
- To be the person you meet for the professional reviews of your progress every half-term, and with whom you review and revise your objectives. They should also make a written record of the progress towards your objectives and discuss with you what new objectives should be set.
- To provide your summative assessment. This will be a judgement as to whether you have successfully reached the standards relevant to that stage of your induction and will take place in the termly assessment meetings at the end of each of the first two terms.
- To keep dated copies of reports of all observations, review meetings and objectives and to make sure you receive copies too.

- To be involved in the final summative assessment at the end of the induction period.
- To evaluate your progress towards and against the standards, and provide constructive feedback and professional development opportunities so that you can improve your performance and reach the required standards.

YOUR ENTITLEMENTS

In England and Wales schools must give you:

- a ten per cent lighter timetable
- a position that does not make unreasonable demands
- regular meetings with your school induction tutor
- a tailor-made programme of support, monitoring and assessment
- objectives to assist you in meeting the induction standards
- at least one observation of your teaching each half-term, with written feedback
- half-termly reviews of your progress
- information of the procedures to raise concerns at school and at higher levels
- an assessment meeting and report at the end of each term.

The DfES and the Welsh Assembly Government (WAG) stress that it is your responsibility to act as quickly as possible if you are not satisfied with any aspect of your induction. In the first instance, raise your concerns with your school, using the internal procedures for raising professional concerns. Raising concerns can be worrying and intimidating even for experienced teachers, so it will probably be more so for you during your induction year. Before raising concerns with your school, it is advisable to seek advice from your union branch secretary or head office.

According to the General Teaching Council of Scotland and The Scottish Executive Education Department, NQTs in Scotland are entitled to:

- a ten per cent lighter timetable
- the support of an induction tutor, who oversees the whole programme and involves other colleagues as and when appropriate
- a minimum of one formal NQT lesson observation per half-term
- a termly review meeting between the induction tutor and the NQT
- termly formal assessment, indicating whether the NQT is meeting the Induction Standards
- NQT to see observation comments
- NQT to sign assessments
- career Entry and Development Profile targets to be negotiated
- targets to form basis for the induction programme
- targets to be reviewed and re-negotiated termly.

YOUR FIRST DAY

When you walk into school for the first time as a teacher, you will feel the same apprehension as a new year 7 pupil. It's a big place and the crush of humanity can be quite claustrophobic. But whereas a new year 7 pupil will be told exactly what to do and when, you will be expected to know instantly what to do and how to do it.

The first day in any job comes with a multitude of stress factors which can never really be completely removed, from simple questions such as "where are the staff toilets?" to far more in-depth issues which more experienced teachers tackle without a second thought.

It is always a sensible idea to go into your new school prior to the first day. This gives you an opportunity to check out your classroom (if you have been designated one; some NQTs find that they have to move between several classrooms). Discuss with your head of department (HoD) a suitable time to meet and discuss what you will need to do (most HoDs will be agreeable to this... hopefully!) and whether you can decorate or re-arrange your new classroom. If you have been allocated a classroom, the general opinion is that it is yours and you can arrange it how you wish. It is always sensible to discuss seating arrangements with your HoD or NQT induction tutor as they can often have suggestions and tips that will be useful. Also, find out about making your own displays and displaying posters which are appropriate for your subject.

Finding out the protocol for the stationery or stock cupboard is essential. Your department may have its own supplies or the school may have one person who controls the flow of supplies. One piece of equipment that is considered essential (and is guaranteed to go walkabout if you lend it to anyone) is a staple gun; try to get yourself one when stationery is ordered, or buy your own and guard it with your life. (You will find that in your career as a teacher you will spend some of your own money on supplies, especially stickers, stationery and posters.)

As the school year progresses, you will find that the students will produce work that is ideal for displays so, for the start of the year it may be an idea to keep things simple. (Eg. if you are an English teacher and know you are going to be teaching the novel "*Holes*" by Louis Sacher, you could find a copy of the movie poster and display it.)

You will find that going into school some time during the last few weeks of the summer holidays will help to ease your anxiety and nervousness about finally having your own classroom and will help you to get into "teacher mode".

Are you familiar with the school day? Do you know when break, lunch and home time are? The best thing you can do is to make a note of it in your day planner for the first few weeks, along with your lesson outlines. You can guarantee that you will not win any friends if you release the students too early or too late.

Have you a basic understanding of the school's layout? Can you at least get to your teaching room? Your first day should be an opportunity for you to walk around. Make use of the maps that most schools hand out to the new intake, just don't let the pupils see you doing it. Don't ask a child for directions as you may end up in the wrong time zone and leave your class waiting outside your room: yet another great way of not making friends.

Do you know the surnames of your colleagues in your department? It would be a good idea to try to remember the names of those colleagues you are going to deal with on a daily basis; other names will come in time. You will be amazed at how fast you will learn them.

Students' names are a bit more of a headache. If you teach five lessons a day, then about 150 students will come in and out of your room. There is no way you can remember all their names. You will remember the troublesome ones, and possibly the talented ones, but most of the rest will remain a blur. A seating plan can help you immensely; you will be able to call each child by name because you will know where he is sitting by consulting your seating plan.

How often are you going to face a problem you cannot answer? Get used to it; there are plenty of questions you will be asked that you won't be able to answer. It doesn't matter if you are an NQT or a long-serving staff member, but what does differ is how you react. In all situations honesty is the best policy. Don't try to bluff your way through, as the students will know instantly. They will have a lot more respect if you simply tell them that you cannot answer that question right now, but will address it again in the next lesson. This gives you time to find out a suitable answer for the next session.

Many schools operate on this kind of basis. There will be some form of morning briefing for staff, and introductions may be made at them. If you are really lucky and are starting at the very beginning of the academic year, then your first day is probably going to be an inset day. This will give you the opportunity to get to know the basic layout of the school and, more importantly, your teaching room.

WHAT TO WEAR IN THE CLASSROOM

It may sound superficial, but what you wear can have as much of an impact on your classroom management as your lesson preparation and behaviour strategies.

We dress to impress in job interviews, so why not for our students, who, if we were translating this to the corporate world, would be our "clients".

Teacher recruitment agencies advocate the sensible approach to work wear, although, as most teachers have experienced from glancing around the staffroom in the morning, people's ideas of appropriate clothing can differ widely.

Back in 1915, there was a politician-inspired code of dress for female teachers in London, which demanded that,

> *"...you may not dress in bright colours, you may, under no circumstances, dye your hair and you must wear at least two petticoats, and dresses must be no shorter than two inches above the ankles".*

While this dress code of 1915 seems scandalous nowadays, female teachers need to be especially careful with what they wear. Cleavage, legs and spaghetti straps are not a good idea if you want to manage a class of testosterone-fuelled boys.

It is safer to dress conservatively; shirt and tie for men and trousers or skirt for women. Women have more flexibility with what they can wear, much to their male colleagues' frustration, but as a general rule women should avoid any clothing that is low-cut, low-rise, too short or see-through. This may seem obvious, but you would be surprised by what some teachers wear to work.

While it is tempting to try and be trendy to relate better to your students, it is advisable to leave clothes that are too tight, too fashionable or made of leather for the weekend.

"If you owned a business, you wouldn't meet your potential clients wearing jeans and a t-shirt, which is unfortunately what some teachers wear to school. Students are our clients and we need to look professional. If we don't, why would the students think us worthy of their respect?" Terrie R, History Teacher, Ipswich.

Top tips

- Avoid low-cut tops, hipster-style pants, strappy tops and short skirts.
- Jeans, trainers and hats should be reserved for mufti or professional development days.
- Anything too fashionable may prove a distraction.
- Conservative doesn't have to mean boring. You can infuse a bit of your own personality with accessories and jewellery.
- Wear nothing that is too tight.
- Wear comfortable clothes and shoes. Fussy clothing and shoes will only hinder your movement around the classroom.
- Trying too hard to be 'cool' is embarrassing for you and your students.
- If you don't feel comfortable with what you are wearing, there's a good chance your students won't either.
- Make sure you are well covered, especially if you have tattoos or piercings.
- Use your common sense when it comes to clothes.

TEACHING

"Brilliant teachers aren't born, they are made", Karen K, Head Teacher, Essex.

There is a great deal of truth in this. Most people will know that they want to be educators long before they become teachers. Let's face it, there are a lot of easier and better-paid jobs out there, so why become a teacher?

The training experienced by a new student teacher has developed a new generation of practitioners which is far more adept and focussed than in the past. The old adage of "Those who can, do; those who can't, teach" is no longer relevant. Ongoing training and career development have made the new generation of teachers highly qualified. Consider this: it takes three years as an undergraduate, a further year following either a PGCE (Post Graduate Certificate of Education) or GTP (Graduate Teaching Programme) route into teaching and then an NQT, or what used to be called a probation year, before you get your DfES number and QTS. It takes a medical student that long to become a junior doctor. So don't ever think that you are not either suitably qualified or a professional.

We are all here to teach, so no matter what else you might be called to do, your primary role is that of educating students. How can you do this?

There are many differing opinions regarding teaching and the theory of teaching. What is the difference between educating and teaching? How do you plan your lesson so that it is not too hard for some, just right for most and hard enough for the minority? How do you structure your lesson and when do you do simple things like take a register or hand out homework?

We will start with the idea of educating rather than teaching. This example dissects this concept perfectly.

> *'A girls' school was having serious problems with some girls who continually put lipstick marks on every mirrored surface they could find. This was taking the caretaker far too long to clean on a daily basis and was obviously also a health hazard, so the headteacher decided to take things in hand. Warnings about the health hazard had no effect on the girls so she took the five most likely culprits into the toilet block along with the caretaker. She then had the caretaker dip his mop into one of the toilets and then use it to clean the mirror. Funnily enough the problem ended overnight".*

This is the difference between teaching (e.g. the health warnings) and educating (the mop).

We can't always achieve a clear distinction between teaching and educating; the main role of teachers today is to get their pupils through public examinations and this has had a direct effect on the way we teach. You may remember your own teachers discussing exams with you and training you to get through them, normally by using old exam papers and working on questions that were likely to turn up in the exam. How much of this information have you actually been able to retain as an adult and, more importantly, when you walked into the exam hall how much of it was available to you?

It is difficult to get the balance between teaching your classes how to pass an exam and teaching them what they need to know. Again, many might say that what they need to know is whatever gets them through the exam, but how much of it will they be able to recall or put into practice later? Make your teaching relevant to your students in their everyday lives, and their ability to recall it in later years or in the exam hall will be dramatically increased.

Now the real problem: the pressure placed on schools and teachers to get their pupils to pass exams and achieve the benchmark five grades at A–C is immense; you cannot fault a teacher who trains their students, because the only recognised system of grading a school's ability to educate children is a very cold set of statistics and these can be interpreted in many different ways.

If you try to make the lesson accessible to the pupils and give them something to really think about, then you will get some of the information to stay in their minds for later recall.

The perennial problem (and one the saving graces of the comprehensive system) is the wide variety of ability levels within any given class, even in groups which are set. There is a simple method you can employ which may enable you to visualise the learning mind-set of people and help you to set work as effectively as you can. We don't claim it works all the time, but it is a good visual reminder.

VYGOTSKY'S ZONE OF PROXIMAL LEARNING

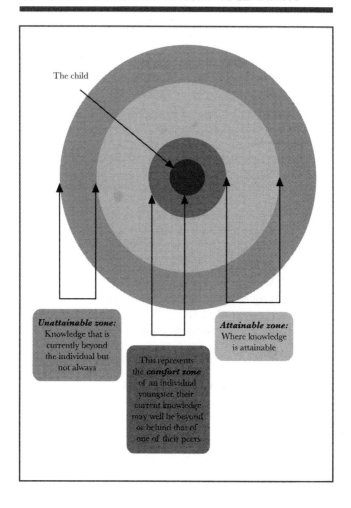

The child

Unattainable zone:
Knowledge that is
currently beyond
the individual but
not always

This represents
the *comfort zone*
of an individual
youngster, their
current knowledge
may well be beyond
or behind that of
one of their peers

Attainable zone:
Where knowledge
is attainable

The concept is based around the visualisation of the child as the centre of the zone, and moving out you can see that each section represents a stage of learning that may or may not be immediately relevant to the individual child. This does not take into account the wide levels of ability you will encounter in the classroom, but it does hold true for everyone: we all have zones of easily-attainable knowledge and knowledge or information that becomes harder to either understand or grasp clearly.

This visual reminder helps to set a lesson plan into context. Consider the child to be the centre of the diagram and then consider the sum of their knowledge which is in the comfort zone before coming to your lesson. You can see that if you place the lesson at too high a level, the weaker students will be at a considerable disadvantage. They will lose interest rapidly, leading to the inevitable disruption of the class as they find other activities to focus their attention on. If you try to set the level too low, then the more able students will become restless. All children are different and the level of knowledge within their comfort zone will be varied. For example:

- **Child A:**
- Comfort zone: All the times tables and fractions
- Attainable zone: Algebra
- Unattainable zone: Simultaneous equations

- **Child B:**
- Comfort zone: The first five times tables
- Attainable zone: Long multiplication
- Unattainable zone: Algebra

This is where differentiation comes into play and why the three-part lesson is an effective method of delivering the curriculum. A good way of ensuring that the whole class learns effectively is to have a number of short activities within the main part of the lesson and then set time limits on them. You must have realistic expectations of the whole group as well as the individuals within it.

The use of differentiation within lessons will enable you to pitch the lesson correctly to each of your classes. A basic starter activity can be used to get the students thinking. This in turn leads into your main activity where the most learning will occur for the majority of the class. For those who are at a higher level, the use of an extension activity will keep them interested and involved in the lesson.

CLASSROOM MANAGEMENT

It seems a little unfair for teachers to have to deal with so many issues not directly related to their main task. But that, of course, is teaching. Behaviour management and classroom management are issues which a lot of people outside education associate with teachers, rather than with their primary roles as educators. There is no single best route to complete control of the learning environment.

The ideal lesson where thirty students sit, obey and hang on to your every word is something you will probably never encounter in your long teaching career. There are, however, a number of very effective strategies you can use to make your life as a teacher far less uncomfortable than it otherwise might be.

A good lesson starts before the students are even in your room. Make sure you are fully prepared for the lesson you are about to give. Use your teacher's planner or, if you still prefer, make use of a lesson plan pro-forma. If you know clearly what you want to happen, then you are going to be far more at ease and this will be picked up by the pupils. Confidence without arrogance is a good way to describe how you should appear, even if it's really like a swan swimming: calm and serene on top while kicking furiously underneath.

Where possible, greet your class at your door. Don't let them in until they are calm. You can do this by insisting that they line up in two rows, one for boys, the other for girls. When you have trained your class, you can have them line up in register order.

Once you are happy with the way they have arrived, welcome them in. Let them go to their assigned chairs and, if you wish, wait until they are told to sit.

How you seat your students in the classroom is vitally important. Very often, it is a trial and error process. However, there are things that you can do to make your job easier. There are various schools of thought on the best way to seat students and the layout of the classroom. Of course, it will take time to get to know students so, at the very start you could consider:

- Seating alphabetically in boy-girl order (if you are in a mixed school).
- Consulting with form tutors or other teachers about good or potentially explosive combinations.
- Letting the students decide in the first instance. This is controversial, but as you are going to want (and need) to change students around, it places responsibility with them straight away and will make it easier to get the seating exactly as you want it later on.

In terms of actual layout of the classroom, it all depends on the size of your room and the subject you teach as to what will work for you. The most common table arrangements are:

- Rows – the advantage of this style is that all students will be facing the front of the classroom. This layout does not always allow for easy movement around the room so you may feel "stuck" up at the front.
- Horseshoe – this style can facilitate easy movement for the teacher, but students can get distracted when facing each other across the room.
- Groups – putting students in groups is great for some kinds of work, but it can prove to be difficult to get students' attention and can create a very noisy atmosphere.

Consult your induction tutor, HoD or simply speak to other teachers and your fellow NQTs in the staff room (or at the pub) and find out what works for them. Some schools actually have policies on seating arrangements (eg. boy-girl) so it is wise to find this out before you make any plans. Some of you will be teaching students that are set; others will be in a mixed ability classroom. You need to seat students in a manner that will best facilitate their learning. This may mean that you seat a less able student next to one who is more able, or a child who finds it hard to settle next to one who could prove to be a calming influence.

It is going to take time to get to know your students, especially if you only see them once or twice a week, and the seating arrangements for your classroom will be something that you will need to change regularly for behaviour management and to facilitate effective teaching.

It is a good idea to designate an area for them to place their bags; there is nothing more embarrassing than falling over a casually-dropped bag. Before the lesson itself begins, ensure that the students have their pencil cases and anything else that they need, as this will minimise the need to fidget or rummage through bags.

A very clear introduction to the lesson is essential and many teachers use the register as a method of calling the class to complete order. It is wise to have a question or activity planned for the class to complete while you take the register, although that may mean that some won't answer their names as they are preoccupied. This won't be too much of a problem once you know the class well and can take the register by sight rather than roll call.

If the students have a clear understanding of what is expected in the lesson, then you will have fewer problems. Make the initial activities simple and short before you get onto the main section of the lesson. A good rule to follow is the three part lesson: introduction, activity and plenary.

As the lesson progresses, don't remain behind your desk; circulate through the class and offer quiet assistance or encouragement where it is due.

The raised eyebrow or pointed look can sometimes be enough to stop any off-task problems and is a very good starting point when dealing with minor behaviour issues. If you are circulating through the class, it may be that you are near the problem or are at least able to get to it with the minimum of fuss. If the stare doesn't work, then the next step is a quiet word with the offender(s).

Removing a student from the room can in itself cause you a great deal of trouble. If the student leaves when asked, then the issue can be dealt with instantly. However, most students will proclaim their innocence or simply try to argue with you, thus disrupting the whole class and placing you in confrontation with an audience who will really enjoy the show. How do you deal with this? One simple statement, such as "leave the room" or "wait outside thank you" may help, but is not a panacea. Never argue or try to justify yourself to the student. Schools have a code of conduct and a series of sanctions which many of the regular troublemakers will know far better than you. Use them carefully and don't make threats. If you need help, seek it from colleagues close to you. Normally, HoDs will be able to solve a lot of problems as they have more authority than the average front-line teacher.

Never shout at or try to make a student look foolish: this will simply increase the level of disruption and lead to further confrontation. If the student is confrontational, raises their voice or gesticulates, remain calm and ask them why they are being so aggressive or simply point out that, although you are both in a confrontation situation, you have not even raised your voice.

Top tips

- Always plan your lessons and ensure that you have the resources you need at hand.
- Ensure that the students are calm before they come into your room.
- Greet the students at the classroom door.
- Don't underestimate the use of simple controls such as the teachers' stare or a quiet word.
- Never try to argue with a student or justify yourself, as this will simply prolong any confrontation.
- Don't use the corridor as a holding bin for offenders. Most of the time they will keep opening the door, ask to come back in and demand to know why they were sent outside. They may also wander off and disrupt other lessons or, worse, engineer a scenario where you send them out of your lesson and thus enable them to meet their friends.
- Make sure you understand the sanctions system your school has in place and use it. Don't rely on a heavy-handed approach.
- Don't threaten anything you cannot or will not do.
- Remain calm at all times and never shout at a student.
- You pick the time and the place to deal with any issues that you think may lead to a confrontation. It is often wisest to have a colleague either present or within earshot, just to be on the safe side.
- Never place yourself in a position where allegations of misconduct can be levelled at you. If you are a male teacher and have a girl on detention make sure you are never alone with her. Better still, have a female member of staff run the detention with or for you. Just make sure you repay the favour.

CALLING HOME

The telephone can be your greatest ally in the ongoing battle that is education today; many parents will be supportive and helpful if you approach them in the right way. It will not help to begin with a negative when dealing with parents or carers. The classic "I am calling because of the appalling behaviour of your child" will not really get the conversation off to a good start. At best, you will get the stock answer "Well, he behaves properly when he's at home" or the conversation may just take a nosedive long before you have the chance to actually get something positive out of the conversation.

Many parents or carers are realistic and know that the most likely place for their children to play up is in the classroom. Try to build a bridge between you and the parent and never apportion blame, as this is ultimately self-defeating. A good approach would be to explain what has happened, inform them of the action you have taken and ask that they reinforce this once the student gets home. Discuss possible sanctions that the parents may wish to use, but try not to be too pushy; think how you would feel if you were the parent and it was your child who was being discussed.

If you are not happy with the 'phone call or feel that the parents have been less than understanding, then speak to the student's head of year and involve them, but remember that you have to set an initial sanction. If the 'phone call degenerates into an unpleasant series of abusive comments from the parent, simply say you are ending the call and hang up. You do not have to put up with abusive people and there are systems in place to deal with these eventualities. Then pass the matter on to a senior member of staff, normally a deputy head, who will then deal with the parent. Make sure you record the call on an incident sheet and state what was said so that the follow-up can be dealt with appropriately.

Top tips

- Remain polite and calm.
- Make a note of whom you call and when.
- Make sure you have any necessary information to hand. You don't want to be left floundering for grades or incident reports.
- Reply to messages as soon as you can.
- If the conversation goes the wrong way, simply end it politely and report it to your line manager, whose job it is to deal with any fallout.

DIPLOMACY

You never thought that diplomacy was also a talent you will have to develop, did you? A strange one to suggest for a teacher, but you will find it a very useful tool, especially if you have to give less than pleasant news to someone. How do you tell students when they have not achieved their target grades? More to the point, how do you tell their parents? A calm and business-like manner does help, but try to remember that schools are not cold sterile places, and those working within them should be able to empathise just a little with their clients.

Parents' evening really does call for a top level of diplomacy, as does report writing (see p. 26). If a student is completely out of control in the class, then most teachers would probably say they were "very lively". If a pupil has not done anything in the time you have taught them, then a simple "has been given every opportunity to engage with the curriculum" will sum up the child in a simple and damning sentence. A few statements which you may want to adopt are:

- Has a great deal of energy that could produce some fantastic work if directed in a suitable and calm manner.
- Has a level of understanding that needs building on if he or she is to progress towards their target grade.
- Needs to direct his or her focus clearly on each task as set.

Top tips

- Be prepared. Have all the information you need to hand.
- Talk to, not at, people and don't use educational jargon or abbreviations if you can avoid it. Many parents or carers will not know what they mean.
- Be as positive and sensitive as you can be when dealing with issues.

TIME MANAGEMENT

Good organisation and time management are some of the most vital skills that you will need as a teacher, especially when, as an NQT, you are establishing yourself in a new school and working your way through new curriculum, materials and schemes of work. If you are not organised you will find that your performance in the classroom (and your quality of life outside it) will suffer.

The government has recognised the need to help teachers manage their time more effectively and achieve a better work-life balance, so it has introduced guaranteed PPA time. This allocates every teacher in every school a guaranteed ten per cent planning, preparation and assessment time by September 2005. By doing this the government hopes to allow teachers to have time to plan and prepare high quality lessons which meet the needs of every pupil.

The way schools organise PPA time will vary, but it is a government requirement and schools must comply or risk the wrath of the teachers' unions.

During your NQT year you will feel, at times, as if you were drowning in a sea of paperwork, marking and lesson plans. You will also bring enthusiasm and fresh ideas to the classroom, although this will take time as you build up your lesson plans and resources.

Decide what works best for you; doing your planning and marking at school or at home. Many experienced teachers swear by the "don't take work home" rule, but as an NQT this can be unrealistic. Separating work and home when you are a teacher can take a few years of practice.

> *"The best advice I got on planning and managing my workload was that I didn't have to reinvent the wheel; beg, borrow and steal any ideas, resources and schemes of work so that you can adapt them." Brigid W, English teacher, NW London.*

Top tips

- There are plenty of existing schemes of work, school and online resources that can be adapted to suit the needs of your students.
- Talk to your subject mentor about different types of assessment, such as peer marking, students marking their own work or verbal feedback. Using a variety of assessment will keep students on their toes and help ease your marking load.
- Observe other teachers as much as you can. Watch how they manage tasks, such as recording and tracking students' progress. You may pick up organisational tips that will help you in your training and beyond.
- Prioritise activities that are both important and urgent: for example, where other people are waiting for your input or for paperwork.
- Get rid of distractions: for example, put your 'phone on voicemail and clear your desk and classroom of clutter.
- Clear out your pigeon hole every day to stay on top of administration and important notices. Write any dates or information down in school planner and discard documents where necessary. (Recycle these, of course, if your school has a recycling bin.)
- Create an organisation system that works for you, whether it is folders, files or computer-based.
- Do your most difficult or time-consuming tasks when you have the most energy. (There are some tasks that you can do while enjoying a glass of wine in front of the TV.)
- Try to locate yourself in an area free from distractions and interruptions when you are trying to get things done.
- Get enough sleep. You are twice as productive when well-rested as when you are fatigued.

REPORT WRITING

The ongoing monitoring and reporting of a student's progress is one of the most important functions which a teacher will carry out in any given year. These reports often contain vital information which is ignored by both the students and parents. So why do we bother? We have a real responsibility to involve parents in the education process and reports are a very effective method of doing this. It also helps us to ensure that progress can be made and then measured against a set of standard criteria.

However, in education today political correctness is a very real problem for public servants. Teachers often feel coerced into writing reports which they do not see as truthful; some believe that politically correct writing requirements mask many of the very real and important issues that they want to raise. If you consider the child who achieves a great deal and works hard then their report will say: "Works very well, tries hard, is a model pupil" and will often finish with: "Should try to maintain the current high standard".

So it's comparatively easy to write reports for those who make use of their time constructively. But what about the problem child? How are you to describe a pupil who disrupts the class, is lazy, rude and of low ability?

Many schools do not allow negative statements to be written. If this is the case in your school, you need to be sure of expressing the truth in a suitable manner. If you don't, you will have to write your report again, so it's better to show your professionalism and get it right the first time.

Beg, borrow or steal comment banks from your colleagues or department. Ask to read examples of your colleagues' reports (or your NQT tutor or HoD). Your fellow NQTs (if you are not the only one) may have resources that they have gleaned from their PGCE or training courses.

Gone are the days of the openly damning report. Remember that we are not here to undermine the students; quite the opposite. You should aim to make constructive suggestions which reflect the aim of a report, which is to inform parents and open the way for dialogue where appropriate.

A former colleague told us that his teacher had written "is content within his own mediocrity" in his final report. Yet this colleague was a fantastic educator and had inspired a great many students who had gone through his unique classes.

Top tips

- Talk to colleagues who have been writing reports for a long time and use their ideas.
- Read previous examples of reports and adapt them to your personal needs.
- Be honest but not negative. You really don't want to have to write all your reports again. Wherever possible, offer a little hope.
- Write a few reports and then get your line manager or mentor to read through them and give you some feedback.
- Don't leave it until the last minute. Teaching after having spent most of the night writing reports is not fun.
- Try to write a few reports each day, otherwise you start getting stale and make mistakes.

THE CALM APPROACH

"Always remain in control of yourself. You can't always control others, but you can control your own behaviour" Gordon A, Science teacher and head of year, Essex.

In the face of the worst case scenario you must be able to remain calm. Virtually all classroom crises will be resolved long before they become a nightmare for you or your class.

Posture and a non-aggressive approach can defuse a lot of tense situations, but remember you're not a police officer or prison guard. Should things get beyond the level of control where you feel comfortable, then the school's behaviour policy will kick in and you should not be left alone.

Top tips

- Speak in a calm manner when dealing with the incident or student.
- Do not be aggressive; a simple comment like "Have I shouted at you?" or "I am only two feet from you, you don't need to shout" can help.
- It helps not to interrupt if you can avoid it. Let students have their say, so long as they are not being aggressive or verbally abusive.
- Make use of the sanctions or rewards systems in place.
- Use the management structure as a support network. It is there for that purpose, and using it is not a reflection on you as a teacher. All teachers must use it at times during their careers.
- If you really feel that there is a lack of support, then you should talk to your union representative.

SCHOOL POLICY

DUTY

You are required to be at school ten minutes earlier than the children and leave ten minutes after they do. Depending on the size of your school, you will have to perform duty at least once a week, and this will entail you going to your assigned duty area and effectively supervising the pupils. The canteen may seem an easy option, but think of all the mess that needs clearing and the amount of children who will go through there during your duty. The far playground is where you get sent if you have really upset someone in the senior management team; it's freezing cold in the winter and uncomfortably hot in the summer.

Do make an effort to find out when your duties are and remember to do them. It's easy to forget, or to turn up late (often caused by keeping children back after lessons or doing necessary things for yourself), but try not to do it too regularly. If you do, you are likely to be reminded by senior management and it creates feelings of resentment among staff who have to cover for you.

TEACHING A SECOND SUBJECT

You are a subject specialist. But it's highly likely that you will be asked to teach outside your subject area.

There are not enough teachers in the profession at the moment. Most schools have a shortfall of staff which leads to teachers having to deliver lessons in an area other than their degree specialism. It is unlikely that you will be given a key stage 4 class if you are teaching a second non-specialist subject though; normally you will have a lower school class and you will simply follow the curriculum. Nine times out of ten, you will spend more time planning your non-specialist lesson than you will your own normal lessons.

Most schools try to consult staff when it comes to these arrangements. They try to either place you in a subject that you may have at A-level, or in a situation that you may want to develop in your teaching. A way to avoid second subject teaching is not to appear too keen to please in your job interview. Otherwise you may end up with a subject that could make your NQT year harder than ever.

Many people consider this an opportunity to expand their teaching practice in another area of the school, though many staff are not keen at all. It is always best to talk to the staff member responsible for the timetable for your second subject if you are not sure about what is being asked of you, but basically your contract will state that the head teacher can ask you to undertake any reasonable duties within the school day.

Top tips

- Make sure you are fully prepared for each lesson. If there is something you don't understand, go through it with the head of department.
- Don't simply bluff your way through these lessons as the children will know and behave accordingly.
- Make sure that any resources are to hand. It is not the same as working in your own department, so resources may not be as easily available.
- Many schools and Local Education Authorities offer some training, so make sure that you use any help that is offered.
- Don't lose sleep over a non-specialist lesson. The principles of teaching are the same whatever you teach, so just be honest and well prepared

---

COVER LESSONS

If you are lucky and your school follows the guidelines, you shouldn't end up in front of a cover class until the third term of your NQT year. But what happens when you do?

Cover lessons are a continual headache for teachers. You are covering the lessons of a colleague who is away ill or who is not available to teach their own lesson. You are not required to cover a lesson if: the staff member is away ill for more than three days (although you do have to do cover during the first three days); the absence is known in advance (ie. school trips or meetings); there is a cover supervisor or agency teacher available. The details of policy within schools and nationally are available to you through union representatives and the DfES web site.

Normally you are supplied with cover work and all you have to do is supervise the class. There is now a growing number of cover technicians who are employed by schools to try to remove as much of the burden from front-line staff as possible.

In September 2005 a real change in the working life of teachers was implemented by the government. This guarantees that ten per cent of teachers' time is now fully protected and cannot be directed by the head teacher. PPA time is to be used by the teacher in whatever manner they should choose; this can include marking, planning or display. No school can ask or require a teacher to cover lessons or attend meetings in their PPA time. They also cannot say what should happen in that time or police it. A further minimum ten per cent of an NQT's reduced (ninety per cent) timetable must be assigned as guaranteed PPA time.

Top tips

- Keep a note of how much cover you do. If it seems excessive, then you can get your head of department to take it up with senior management.
- Good supply teachers always have backup lessons and resources. Have a few basic worksheets handy, just in case. (Generic word searches or crosswords always go down well.)
- If the cover work that is set seems inadequate, make a note of it for the teacher.

HOMEWORK

Your school's homework policy will explain clearly how often homework is to be set and on which days it is to be set and due to be given in. Most departments have their own policy, based on the expectations of the school.

The perennial headache for teachers is how to enforce the homework policy. How do you set it, at what point in the lesson do you set it and how do you collect it in?

You can ruin the feel of a lesson if you spend time collecting the homework in, especially if you have a large number of pupils which does not comply with the work set. Some schools also do random checks of homework (usually undertaken by senior staff) to check on which staff members do (or more importantly, do not) set homework routinely.

Top tips

- Write the homework on the board and ensure that every student writes it in their diaries. Some of the children will need it writing in by you or a trusted peer.
- Stop the whole class at a convenient point and ensure that your expectations are made clear.
- Always remain consistent, set the work at the same time every lesson and have a standard hand-in time.
- Don't discuss any issues with non-compliance during the lesson; you should have the child come back in their time. Be very aware of the fact that any time outside of lessons is also your time, so plan carefully when and if you wish to have a child come back to you.
- It is a good idea to have a homework book which the students leave on their desks open to the current page. During the lesson you can move through the room, assist with any problems and give the books the once-over before you collect them in at the end of the session for a more detailed assessment.

DEPARTMENTAL POLICY

This is the area where you are going to spend the majority of your time and where you are going to develop your teaching practice. It is important to make sure you are very clear about the department's policies and schemes of work schemes of work. The policy will be the responsibility of the head of department, but most tend to leave policy up to open discussion and choose the area or departmental meetings as an opportunity to develop it.

Most schools have a series of policies that cover the running of the school and its departments. This will include what schemes of work are used, when homework is set, how often books should be marked (sometimes even how they should be marked), lessons and formats. We shall go through these one at a time.

SCHEMES OF WORK

You are very unlikely to enter a school as an NQT and have no resources to hand. The schemes of works will have been developed over a number of academic years, slowly being refined into a workable and effective method of ensuring the whole curriculum can be delivered at all key stages. Many people are happy to share their ideas, and you should really take advantage of this if you have any problems. There are also a number of web sites that offer free schemes of works which you can take and develop to suit yourself.

MARKING

Marking is the bane of a teacher's life. However, it is important to ensure progress by showing students how well they are doing and what expectations you have of them. There are two main forms of assessing students used in schools today: summative and formative. Summative assessment covers the marking of completed work giving a finished grade, while formative is an ongoing assessment and can be given verbally or set as targets.

Your whole school will have a marking policy. This will set down the expectations of how often, and sometimes how, books will be marked (eg. effort grades and National Curriculum levels). It will also include basic instructions, like not using red pens (some schools prefer green) when marking or making a positive comment at the end of each section that is marked.

Top tips

- Stick a list in the front of your students' books so that they, their parents and others know how the books are marked.
- Keep on top of your marking. The more regularly you mark books, the less of a mountainous task it seems.
- Avoid collecting in key stage 3 books at the end of half-terms, as this is usually when you need to mark coursework.
- Use peer assessment. This can cut down your marking dramatically. It also gives students responsibility for their learning and assessment.
- Use stickers and stamps. There is a plethora of sticker companies which provide excellent target stickers and stamps for overworked teachers. This can save you time, and students love getting stickers and stamps on their work.

BEHAVIOUR

The behaviour issue is one that has many experts scratching their heads, while some parents and MPs call for a return of the cane or more permanent exclusions. It's interesting to note that if one school excludes a student permanently, then another school has to take them in. All that happens is that the problem is moved elsewhere and is not actually solved. If you talk to a lot of teachers, the vast majority would not really want to see a return to the days of corporal punishment. So what do we do about these serious problems (officially termed as low-level disruptors)? There are no simple solutions, although many colleagues have been kind enough to share their experiences.

A simple and really effective starting point is:

> *"With your form group or the class you teach, find out the story behind the more troublesome pupils. This may help you understand why they behave the way they do." Georgie C, Former school librarian and now graduate teacher programme student.*

This will not solve any issues but it may help you to at least understand why the students behave as they do for you. It's never a personal thing, they don't hate you. The students simply don't like what you represent, and for some you are the only adult who can be trusted to be fair and honest. You are a safe adult who the students know will always be there.

As teachers we try to instil a sense of routine and formality upon many students who have never experienced it before. Many children are told "no" at home by parents who then do not enforce it, yet at school teachers will always carry out what they promise. This is the first area in which students and teachers come into conflict. The best possible policy to follow is that of consistency. Always do what you say you are going to do. Most often that will be either a detention or ringing the student's parents. Never underestimate the effect this may have on some of the students you teach. They may be perfect at home and demons at school.

Top tips

- Get to know your pupils' first names in order to personalise the communication and give you, as the teacher, a sense of control. This can be difficult of you only see a class once a week, so have a seating plan handy for easy reference.
- Use non-verbal cues such as hand signals or movements to indicate what you want the class to do.
- Use positive directions such as "want" and "need". These are more assertive that "I would like". Also, thank the students when they answer a question or when you want them to do something. Don't use "please" with them. "It's time to settle down, thanks" is stronger than "It's time to settle down, please."
- Pause between using the student's name and giving an instruction. This helps to focus the student.
- Make sure you are familiar with your school's code of conduct and behaviour policy (eg. sanctions, use of referral room).
- Model the kind of behaviour that you want in the classroom. This can be really hard, but remaining calm and controlled is better than shouting and screaming at a student or class.
- It's not wrong to apologise to a child if you have been unfair to them (this will happen in your career). Take the student aside quietly and talk to them, explaining that you are human too and can make mistakes. More often than not, the child will feel better and it will help to develop your relationship with him or her.

- Separate the behaviour from the child. For example, instead of saying "you are silly or rude" let them know that the behaviour is not appropriate eg. "your behaviour is very silly at the moment" or "the way you have just spoken to me is very rude..." and follow up with a sanction or consequence.

- Be consistent and follow through on the issues that matter.

- Remember, behaviour management takes time. You will not have it cracked straight away, it is an ongoing process.

SPECIAL EDUCATIONAL NEEDS

A very handy port of call for any teacher is the SENCO (Special Educational Needs Coordinator). This is the member of staff who deals with children with learning difficulties; these will include children with both educational and emotional problems. The wealth of knowledge most SENCOs have is well worth tapping. They are, after all, the school's experts when it comes to behavioural difficulties. Many of the children they are responsible for have any of an array of problems, which can be bewildering to the non-specialist. It is a well-known fact that, as children become older and fall further behind their peers or are unable to cope with the work, then the behavioural problems will become accentuated. It won't help simply to differentiate in lessons, especially if they feel that you are giving them simple tasks because you think they are not capable of completing the more complex work their peer group is undertaking. Talk to the SENCO and to the LSAs. As they deal with these children on a day-to-day basis, they will know them far better than you will, and may be able to help you in planning effective methods of delivering lessons to them.

Here are some of the more common learning disorders you are likely to have to deal with on a daily basis:

Attention Deficit Hyperactivity Disorder

This is a very controversial topic; many children with learning difficulties also have concentration difficulties. It is very important to ensure that there are no other factors within the child such as anxiety, depression or adverse family situations which might be affecting their activity and concentration levels. Poor parenting skills are common in a very high proportion of these cases. The most commonly used medication for children with attention deficit hyperactivity disorder (ADHD) is Ritalin, which is a stimulant. This may seem an odd choice for treating hyperactive children because stimulants increase activity in the brain and normally make people more alert and active. However, stimulants at the doses used for ADHD have the opposite effect. Ritalin is controversial and not all the students that you teach who have been diagnosed with ADHD will take it.

Many children on Ritalin will need to take it during the school day. In summary, the DfES document *Managing Medications in Schools and Early Years Settings* (2005) outlines that:

- Any member of staff may administer a controlled drug to the child for whom it has been prescribed.
- Staff administering medicine must do so in accordance with the prescriber's instructions.
- It is permissible for schools to look after a controlled drug, where it is agreed that it will be administered to the child for whom it has been prescribed. Schools should keep a controlled drug locked in a non-portable container and only named staff should have access.
- A record should be kept for safety and audit purposes.

Ritalin (Methylphenidate) in Schools – A Briefing Paper (Drug and Alcohol Education and Prevention Team, 2005)

It is unlikely that you will be called upon to administer a drug like Ritalin to a child. There will probably be an arrangement with the school office where the student will go at a designated time to take their medication.

Asperger's syndrome

Asperger's syndrome is a form of autism with the most common traits being difficulty in communicating, difficulty in social relationships and a lack of imagination and creative play. Unlike austistic children, those with Asperger's syndrome have fewer problems with language and are often of average or above-average intelligence.

Dyslexia

This term is applied to children who have specific learning difficulties and this may affect a number of areas, not just reading.

Dyspraxia

Children with impairment of executive and organisational motor functions. Sometimes it is accompanied by other difficulties such as attention deficit, tick syndromes or mild autism.

It is always sensible to know whether a child is on medication (eg. insulin, Ritalin, EpiPen) so that in the event of any medical incidents or emergencies in the classroom, you will be aware of what you are dealing with and can call for the appropriate help.

PHYSICAL DISABILITY

With the emphasis on inclusion in education, it is highly likely that you will teach students with physical disabilities.

The Special Educational Needs and Disability Act 2001 created important new duties for schools and local authorities. Schools must take "reasonable steps" to ensure that disabled pupils are not greatly disadvantaged (more so than their disability dictates) in relation to the education and other services they provide. This means they must plan ahead, identify barriers to learning and, as far as possible, take action to remove them; schools are also required to draw up accessibility plans.

Check through the medical notes in a school and you will find many students who have diabetes, allergies that require the use of an EpiPen (administers adrenaline in the event of severe allergic reactions) and epilepsy. You will also find that you teach students with various conditions ranging from sickle cell anaemia to degenerative diseases, which means the student has limited communication skills.

Students with physical disabilities differ in the support they need for their studies. Some secondary schools have specialist learning development departments, which means that there are a greater proportion of students with physical disabilities that require both specialist learning support and physical therapy.

As a teacher you have responsibility for:

■   ensuring disabled people are not treated less favourably.
■   making reasonable adjustments to courses, teaching or the environment, as required.

This may seem like an insurmountable task, but all students with a physical disability, whether it's cerebral palsy, visual impairment, muscular dystrophy or cystic fibrosis (to name just a few of the conditions that you may encounter in your teaching career) will have designated learning support.

On its website, the Disability Rights Commission advises that:

> *"Teachers with disabled students in their class are advised to meet them informally before the lessons so that they can find out their wishes. They may want to take a direct role in the class and feel comfortable about answering questions and sharing life experiences, or they may not wish to be marked out in this way. The discussion with the disabled students and the lessons need to be handled sensitively. Teachers need to know about the school's confidentiality policies, and the rights of disabled students in education..."*
> *(www.drc-gb.org).*

Your school's SEN department should be able to provide you with advice on how to cater for any students with disabilities who you will be teaching. It is also worth looking at the revised *SEN Code of Practice* (2002), which provides a framework for schools and LEAs, among others, on carrying out their statutory duties to identify, assess and make provision for children's SEN. Your school will have a copy of this.

BEHAVIOURAL, EMOTIONAL AND PHYSICAL SUPPORT

1. Any child who has a full statement should have permanent help from an LSA, who will accompany him or her to every lesson. As you might imagine, this is a very expensive problem for a lot of schools.
2. If a student is classed as "school action" or "school action +" then he or she will have help in key lessons, normally Maths, English and Science, although it may not be for every lesson. In many cases he or she will not have continual support but will from time to time be dealt with by the SEN team as a method of monitoring.
3. Some children have emotional issues which may cause problems in lessons for teachers, but they will not normally have a full time LSA
4. Other students may have a physical disability which can range from mild to very severe. Depending on the severity of the disability they may have a full time LSA.

Top tips

- Remain calm at all times. You may notice that this is one of the most common tips we give, but it's also one of the best.
- Refer to the information given to you through the SEN department or from previous schools. All junior school children will have a written report sent to the secondary school they attend.
- Talk to more experienced members of staff; see what they do and how they do it.
- Observe as many lessons as your NQT timetable permits, get a wide range of experience watching other teachers at work.
- Attend any courses that your LEA or school run, as they will really help you get a good understanding of how to deal with difficult students or situations.
- If you have a problem which you cannot deal with, don't forget that every other teacher will have gone through a very similar set of problems when they started out. Today we understand a lot more about how to offer support, and you should never be afraid to ask for help if you need it.
- Above all, always be consistent and fair.

WORKING WITH TEACHING ASSISTANTS

This section will help you to get the most out of the support provided. Depending on your school's staffing arrangements and the number of children on roll with SEN or English as an additional language (EAL) requirements, you will probably have learning support in your classroom and you should be very grateful for it. As you will discover, good learning support is a tremendous help in the classroom.

Establishing a good working relationship with learning support assistants (LSAs) is vital for the smooth running of your classroom. This will depend very much on the particular LSA's personality and working style and whether this is compatible with yours.

Top tips

- Some teachers get a bit intimidated when an learning support assistant (LSA) is in their class. Good LSAs often watch teachers closely in order to pick up teaching tips, so don't get too paranoid if you feel as if you are being observed by them.
- Use their expertise. Many LSAs are well versed in, for example, English texts studied and often have fantastic resources built up over the years from the various teachers they have supported. They are also an invaluable resource for differentiated worksheets and activities.
- Delegate. You need to delegate to make your life easier and also to give the LSA an opportunity to be really active in their particular responsibilities, whether it be for a particular child or for the class as a whole. Some LSAs will be very self-motivated and proactive; others will take more of a passive role and need a lot of direction from you.

- Communicate. Ideally you could find a time to meet LSAs to discuss a particular class or a student's specific needs and to give them guidance on the direction that should be taken.

- Try to give LSAs your lesson plans or resources in advance so that they can adapt to suit the students in your class requiring support. It can seem like the last thing on your mind when you are swamped with lesson preparation, marking and paperwork, but remember, LSAs have a job to do as well and it is one of your many responsibilities to help them perform their duties. This, in turn, will help you to perform better in the classroom.

"The best teachers to work with are ones that include us in the lesson. This is probably easier in humanities-based subjects, but it makes LSAs feel valued and as if they are part of the class. It also helps the students to see the LSA as important, not just the 'teaching assistant'." Sue, Teaching Assistant, Harrow, Middlesex.

BEING A FORM TUTOR

Being a form tutor is one of the most challenging and rewarding responsibilities a teacher will undertake in their career. As an NQT, you may be given a form of your own, but the more likely situation is that you will perform assistant form tutor duties or be attached to a particular form group. The most undesirable situation is to inherit a form group, because it can be very difficult to gain ground with the students if they are not in their first year of high school.

It is a common belief among NQTs and teacher trainees that it is against Teacher Training Agency regulations for you to be a form tutor in your induction year; this is untrue. In theory, it is inadvisable for NQTs to have the added responsibility, but in practice many schools struggle to assign tutors to forms, so it is likely that you will have one. As most teachers will be a form tutor at some stage, it's better to start sooner rather than later.

The time teachers spend with their forms or tutor groups is a vital part of secondary education. Many teachers welcome the opportunity to get to know a group of students well and play an integral part in their education, while others can view form tutor duties as an intrusion on their main role as a subject teacher.

It is important to realise that being a form tutor is not a just an add-on responsibility; it plays an integral part in school life and the whole school experience for a student. Just remember how you felt when you were part of a form. Personal memories and experiences can help shape the kind of form tutor a teacher will become.

The main aim of being a form tutor is to deliver the social side of education to complement the academic learning that occurs in the classroom. As a form tutor, a teacher can counteract the de-motivation and sense of isolation that many students can experience at school.

The role of a form tutor is so vast that it is virtually impossible to define. The only certainty is that you will be required to perform many roles, including communicator, problem-solver, morale-booster, administrator, nurturer, manager of behaviour and, at times, confidant.

BE ORGANISED

Being organised is probably the most important asset for a form tutor. As well as the legal requirement to keep attendance records, as a form tutor you will be expected to deliver important notices about school life. Keep a separate folder for your form group to manage information, records and correspondence from parents or carers. It is also important to have routines. For example, check diaries regularly so that you can keep track of whether students are recording their homework properly. Keep a note of any messages from parents or carers.

LEAD BY EXAMPLE

Arrive on time and keep on top of your duties to set a firm example to your class. Students are led by example, so you will help them to value assets such as punctuality and organisation which are vital for successful education and will establish good habits for later life.

SET THE RULES FROM THE START

This seems obvious, but it is vitally important to lay the ground rules from the very start. This means having a seating plan (you can always change it as the year progresses and you discover the different personalities of your students) and using all the basic behaviour strategies that you would in the classroom. These strategies include waiting for silence before speaking and having a merit and sanction system. It is tempting, especially for new teachers, to try and be a friend to your tutor group and for them to think you are "safe". Remember that your students don't need friends; they already have plenty of them. But you are their only form tutor and should represent a unique position in their school lives. A casual approach to form tutoring (not having a seating plan, having no structure to form time) will lead to more stress and start the day off on a bad footing. It will also store up problems for the future, as all experienced teachers will know. So it is important to make form time matter. Students should know it is an important time of the day, not just a time for the teacher to catch up on marking and subject-related paperwork.

ENCOURAGE OWNERSHIP AND RESPONSIBILITY

Encourage the students to feel a sense of care and ownership of their form room through use of displays, in particular the form board. Encourage student responsibility by getting students to keep the form room tidy, take on various roles like handing out letters and books, get the register from the office, run errands and be responsible for the daily class behaviour and class work record.

KEEP RECORDS

Monitoring attendance is a legal requirement for form tutors and it can also prove valuable in gauging if there are any problems which could be affecting a student's performance. Keeping a track of your form's behaviour and class work in individual subjects is also a powerful tool in performing pastoral duties effectively and ensuring that any problems are addressed. Rewarding your form for good behaviour, both collectively and individually, is also important for motivating students.

MEET THE PARENTS

During the course of the academic year there will be occasions, such as parent-teacher evenings or school functions, when you will meet your students' parents or carers. Establishing a relationship with your form's parents or carers is invaluable in helping to meet your responsibilities and duties as a form tutor.

GETTING TO KNOW YOU

Developing relationships with your students is probably the most vital aspect of being a form tutor. As well as carrying out the administrative duties which must be done each day, you should set aside time to talk to students and get to know what is happening in their lives. You could also establish a regular session like "thought for the day" or discussion of current events locally or internationally. Of course, with issues such as terrorism and war, sensitivity and clear leadership in any discussion is needed to avoid any potentially difficult situations. As a form tutor you may be required to deliver sex education, depending on your school's policy. This also presents an opportunity to discuss with students wider issues of self-esteem, self-care and responsible citizenship and can help establish an environment of trust within a form group.

CO-TUTORS

Co-tutors range from other NQTs to far more experienced colleagues; the opportunity to work alongside a member of staff who knows both the system and, quite probably, the children is a great boon for the new teacher. Many colleagues will be able to provide you with practical and moral support in your first year.

Top tips

- Be organised so that you can keep paperwork under control and meet deadlines.
- Be punctual to set a good example.
- Make sure you are never too busy or too rushed for your students to approach you with a problem.
- Be diplomatic and try not to take sides, even when it is tempting, so that your form knows you will treat them fairly.
- Give your tutor time status and structure. Don't let it become a period that you can use to catch up on your own work, or let students do what they want.
- Be interested in your students and find out about their lives by talking to them, rather than interrogating them for information.
- Emphasise "we" rather than "you" when addressing the form. Use school-based activities to build a sense of teamwork and cooperation.
- Let your form know that you enjoy being with them. If you have a difficult group, try to find ways to engage with them.
- Don't expect all students to like you, but try to be likeable without acting as their "best friend".
- Establish a clear discipline and rewards system so that the form knows there will be consequences for behaviour, both positive and negative.

CHILD PROTECTION

Every school will have a child protection policy and conduct training for staff. As a form tutor, you will be in a better position than most to spot any signs of abuse.

If you have reason to suspect that a child you teach is suffering from any kind of abuse, you should report your concerns to your school's "designated person" – a senior member of the school's leadership team who is designated to take lead responsibility for dealing with child protection issues, providing advice and support to other staff, liaising with the LEA, and working with other agencies.

If you are the first point of contact for a child wishing to disclose, you are a very important person for that particular child.

If this happens, it may be tempting to want to ask lots of questions about the abuse, but this is not your role. The school must find out just enough about the alleged abuse in order to make a decision about a referral.

WHAT IS ABUSE?

Child abuse is a term which describes all the ways in which a child's development and health are damaged by the actions or inactions of others. This usually means actions by adults but it can sometimes be the actions of other children.

There are four categories of child abuse, which often overlap:

- physical abuse
- sexual abuse
- emotional abuse
- neglect.

The UN Convention on the 'Rights of the Child' 1991 states:

"Children have the right to be protected from all forms of violence. They must be given proper care by those looking after them."

WHAT ARE THE SIGNS AND SYMPTOMS OF CHILD ABUSE?

If you suspect child abuse, but aren't sure, look for clusters of the following physical and behavioural signs.

Some signs of physical abuse

- unexplained burns, cuts, bruises, or welts in the shape of an object
- bite marks
- anti-social behaviour
- problems in school
- fear of adults
- drug or alcohol abuse
- self-destructive or suicidal behaviour
- depression or poor self-image.

Some signs of emotional abuse

- apathy
- depression
- hostility
- lack of concentration
- eating disorders.

Some signs of sexual abuse

- inappropriate interest in or knowledge of sexual acts
- seductiveness
- avoidance of things related to sexuality, or rejection of own genitals or bodies
- nightmares and bed wetting
- drastic changes in appetite
- over-compliance or excessive aggression
- fear of a particular person or family member
- withdrawal, secretiveness or depression
- suicidal behaviour
- eating disorders
- self-injury.

Sometimes there are no obvious physical signs of sexual abuse, and a physician must examine the child to confirm the abuse.

Some signs of neglect

- unsuitable clothing for weather
- being dirty or un-bathed
- extreme hunger
- apparent lack of supervision.

EMOTIONAL LITERACY

Emotional literacy (EL) is, in its simplest terms, the ability to recognise, understand, handle and appropriately express emotions. Advocates of emotional literacy believe that success in personal relationships and career has a direct link with an individual's level of emotional intelligence (EI).

EI came into greater public awareness with the 1995 publication of *Emotional Intelligence: Why it can matter more than IQ* by US psychologist Daniel Goleman. Although EL is still a relatively new concept in the education world, many LEAs in the UK are using the ideas from Goleman's text as a springboard to launch initiatives on emotional literacy.

Southampton was the first LEA to launch an EI initiative in 1997, looking first at anger management, then at social skills and self-esteem. Now, EI is becoming integrated into most LEAs, focusing on areas which include learning and achievement, social and health education, spiritual, moral and cultural development, equal opportunities, behaviour and discipline, social inclusion and crime and disorder.

"I try and set aside a lesson every few weeks that focuses on emotional literacy and I use a stimulus, such as a video, picture or newspaper article to promote discussion and thought. It takes a little time to get the students into the routine of an 'EI' lesson but it is well worth it and they feel a sense of ownership over these lessons. Clear it with your HoD first and make sure it fits in with your curriculum. EI is great because it is applicable in all subjects." Tania G, English teacher, NW London

Top tips

- Greet students at the door. Show an interest in them and their lives as individuals.
- Provide verbal questions aimed at a range of ability levels so that all students can be seen by their peers to achieve success.
- When calling out the register, try different strategies like asking students to name a colour to express their emotions at that moment – you will get answers ranging from "black" to "fluorescent pink with green stripes".
- Use pictures, music or poetry to stimulate discussion about feelings.
- Display an inspiring or motivating "quote of the week" in your classroom.
- Start an Emotional Literacy group at school – for staff as well as students. Some schools have started a staff book study of the Daniel Goleman book, *Emotional Intelligence: Why it can matter more than IQ*.
- Use games and role-play to develop students' personal skills.
- Use stories that contain therapeutic metaphors – ideas that the child can identify with to help them change the way they behave. If a vulnerable student perceives the surrounding world as threatening, the most effective intervention may be to challenge that perception.
- Develop your own emotional literacy by reading, continuing professional development or just talking to colleagues.
- You are your best resource. Keep yourself emotionally fit and healthy.

THE CHECKS

UNIFORM

Uniform is the single most common cause of conflict within the classroom. In an environment where you strive to find positives, the uniform issue usually starts with negatives. There are no simple solutions to this perennial problem; patience and consistency are the only real tools at your disposal. Many schools operate a robust uniform policy, with clear rewards and sanctions which make the lives of teachers much easier. In some cases this is not true; you have the hierarchy (refer to the school policy section) to turn to should you encounter problematic or regular breaches of the uniform code.

STUDENT PLANNERS/DIARIES

These are a must for all students. They help them to keep a record of their homework assignments, and will contain a home-school agreement and an internet agreement. It will have room for their timetable and will be lost or ignored by the end of the first week. The students will try to ignore the diary and will forget it as often as they can. Your role as form tutor is to try to keep track of this book and ensure that not only you sign it, but the parents sign it too.

EQUIPMENT CHECKS

Most students will never turn up with the right equipment after the first day. It is not too far-fetched to say that the continual demand for pens or pencils at the start of most lessons is the bane of teachers' lives. You have to think about what you hand out, who has it and then make time to collect it after the lesson. The regular offenders begin to rely on you far too much and will learn who is an easy touch. It is a very annoying to have your lesson interrupted on a regular basis, especially when students should have the equipment anyway.

There are a number of simple steps you can follow which may have some positive effects within the classroom.

- Charge the children a flat fee for buying the equipment they need.
- Take something from a child if they borrow your equipment (a colleague of mine takes a child's shoe).
- You can simply hand out detentions for any child who forgets their equipment.
- You can omit the child from the lesson and set them separate work. This really works if the lesson is practical.
- Simply hand out a detention for non-compliance; you may find that this is actually your department's policy anyway.

These will work in the end, but you have to be consistent and fair in the way you apply the rules. Make no exceptions, even for those who are usually exemplary, and remember that you are helping the students to become self-reliant

DIFFICULT SITUATIONS IN THE CLASSROOM

It is a fact that teachers, just by working with children, are put in a vulnerable position every day of their working lives. Using common sense and good practice can help to avoid or defuse most situations.

STUDENT CRUSHES OR ROMANTIC ATTACHMENTS

From the beginning of time, young people have developed crushes, romantic attachments and sexual longings for people both of their age and older.

If you feel uncomfortable with a pupil's behaviour or infatuation then speak to a senior respected teacher, such as a head of year or deputy head before taking any action. It is probably wise to seek advice on this issue from colleagues or your union before you make any attempt to deal with it in its early stages (ie. explaining to the student why any comments or behaviour are inappropriate).

It is important, however, to let the student know (at a subconscious level mainly) that such feelings do not mean there is anything wrong with them as a person.

THE BRISTOL GUIDE

You should have been given this guide to teachers' legal liabilities and responsibilities during your training. Reading the Bristol Guide satisfies the requirements of Standard 1.8 of the Teacher Training Agency's standards for the award of QTS that *'trainee teachers must be aware of, and work within, the statutory frameworks relating to teachers' responsibilities'*.

REASONABLE USE OF RESTRAINT

A new provision came into force on 1 September 1998 clarifying the powers of teachers, and other staff who have lawful control or charge of pupils, to use reasonable force to prevent pupils committing a crime, causing injury or damage or causing disruption.

The wording of this provision states:

1) *A member of the staff of a school may use, in relation to any pupil at the school **such force as is reasonable in the circumstances** for the purpose of preventing the pupil from doing (or continuing to do) any of the following, namely:*

- *committing any offence*
- *causing personal injury to, or damage to the property of, any person (including the pupil himself); or*
- *engaging in any behaviour prejudicial to the maintenance of good order and discipline at the school or among any of its pupils, whether behaviour occurs during a teaching session or otherwise.*

2) *This applies where a member of the staff of a school is:*

- *on the premises of the school; or*
- *elsewhere at a time when as a member of its staff, he has lawful control or charge of the pupil concerned.*

ALLEGATIONS OF ABUSE (VERBAL, PHYSICAL, SEXUAL)

This is every teacher's nightmare – an allegation of abuse. Teachers are particularly vulnerable to such allegations because of the nature of their job. Sadly, some pupils have no compunction about making false allegations against teachers they dislike.

Unfortunately, a teacher must be suspended from duty during any investigations into allegations (even if false, which in most cases they are) of abuse. Under current legislation, teachers accused of child abuse are always presumed guilty until proven otherwise. It has also been shown that once an allegation has been publicised, even after the teacher has been cleared, dismissal or inability to return to work is almost certain.

Top tips

- Make sure you are never alone with a student. If you are a male teacher and are talking to a female pupil, ensure that the door is open and that there is another student present. This is also very important for female teachers. Avoid situations that leave you alone with a male student.
- Avoid getting involved in breaking up fights, both for your own safety and to avoid a situation where a student can make an allegation of abuse.
- Don't be over-familiar with students. Keep firm boundaries.

GENERAL HANDY HINTS

- Talking to parents can sometimes be a really awful experience especially when dealing with an uncooperative or abusive parent, but remember that there are senior members of staff who can and will help you in such difficult situations.

- Be prepared. If you know what you are going to do, then lessons will be far less stressful for you and the students.

- If you don't know something, be honest and say you can find out. Sometimes you can bluff, but don't think that you will always get away with it.

- Consider what you need for the day ahead and make sure you have it to hand in advance. It's always wise to go to your teaching room before the students arrive so that everything is in order.

- If you need certain things, like projectors or computer rooms, for your lesson, ensure that they are booked well in advance.

- Keep your diary with you, and spend five minutes at the start and end of each day updating it.

- Make sure you know the school's sanctions and, more importantly, rewards systems clearly. Sometimes you will find that key stage 3 and key stage 4 have different systems in place.

- Never devalue what a student has produced. This is the quickest way of turning off students and can lead to many issues which are avoidable in the first place.

- Don't be too proud to say that you need help.

- Experiment with differing approaches and see what works best for you and your classes.

- Remember that some lessons are simply going to crash and burn. Learn from them and move on. Don't brood.

■ Empathise but never sympathise. A good example of this would be: "You see someone who has fallen down a hole, if you sympathise with them you get into the hole and feel what they feel, if you empathise with them you do something to get them out of the hole".

WORKPLACE BULLYING

Hopefully, this is not a problem that you will ever encounter during your career, let alone your NQT year, but it is worth being aware of. Teachers are well-informed about bullying when it comes to students, but less so when it comes to bullying in the staffroom.

Bullying is defined as "the unjust exercise of power of one individual over another by the use of means to humiliate, frighten, denigrate or injure the victim".

In schools where staff bullying does exist, it tends to come mainly from those in positions of power, such as head teachers, deputy heads and heads of year or department.

If you're experiencing bullying, teachers' unions recommend several steps including:

- keeping written records
- complaining to the line manager if he or she is not the bully
- keeping copies of any bullying memos and their replies
- establishing the status of any meeting before agreeing to attend and, where appropriate, being accompanied by someone you trust
- raising the issue with teacher or staff governors
- recording when the incident(s) lead to illness requiring sick leave
- counselling, eg. Teacher Support Line
- contacting your teachers' union.

STAFFROOM POLITICS

It is vital to set off on the right foot and avoid some initial errors. These could make you more enemies in the first five minutes of your career than you are likely to make in the rest of it. Nearly all staffrooms have a political life of their own; you may find that the teachers who have been at the school for a long time have a certain section of the staffroom and the newer staff members have a different one. Make it your business to find out discreetly about any perceived pecking order.

The staff room can be a hotbed of intrigue and influence and in some ways it's far more dangerous than the playground duty you are inevitably going to get as an NQT. It is full of up-to-date gossip and general slander.

> *"I recommend going to the staff room at least once a week for a proper sit-down lunch and not just hiding in your own department. Relaxing is essential at least once a week and the staff room is where the senior management team are found. If you want to progress you need to get to know those in the know." Elizabeth G, Physics teacher, Leicestershire.*

LOOKING AFTER YOURSELF

While not all teachers will suffer from stress-related disorders, teaching is widely regarded as one of the most stressful professions.

Research by the main teachers' union, the National Union of Teachers (NUT) confirms this. A survey in 1999 found thirty-six per cent of teachers felt the effects of stress all or most of the time.

In a 2000 report by the NUT called *Tackling Stress*, the key causes of teacher stress were identified as:

- long working hours
- excessive workload
- pressures of school inspections
- providing cover for teacher shortages and absences
- poor management
- disruptive pupil behaviour
- unnecessary bureaucracy
- low self-esteem
- criticism by politicians and media.

CHECK YOUR STRESS LEVELS

Stress symptoms fall into four categories:

- behavioural (the things you do)
- physical (your body's response)
- emotional (what you feel)
- psychological (your personal thinking style).

Count how many of the symptoms below you are experiencing. Your score at the end will show how stressed you really are.

Physical symptoms

- ❑ tightness in chest
- ❑ chest pain and/or palpitations
- ❑ indigestion
- ❑ breathlessness
- ❑ nausea
- ❑ muscle twitches
- ❑ aches and pains
- ❑ headaches
- ❑ skin conditions
- ❑ recurrence of previous illnesses/allergies
- ❑ constipation/diarrhoea
- ❑ weight loss or weight gain
- ❑ change in menstrual cycle for women
- ❑ sleep problems/tiredness

Emotional symptoms

- ❑ mood swings
- ❑ feeling anxious
- ❑ feeling tense
- ❑ feelings of anger
- ❑ feeling guilty
- ❑ feelings of shame
- ❑ having no enthusiasm
- ❑ becoming more cynical
- ❑ feeling out of control
- ❑ feeling helpless
- ❑ decrease in confidence/self-esteem
- ❑ poor concentration

Behavioural symptoms

❏ drop in work performance

❏ more inclined to become accident-prone

❏ drinking and smoking more

❏ overeating/loss of appetite

❏ change in sleeping patterns

❏ poor time management

❏ too busy to relax

❏ withdrawing from family and friends

❏ loss of interest in sex

❏ poor judgement

❏ inability to express feelings

❏ over-reacting

Psychological symptoms and negative thoughts

❏ 'I am a failure'

❏ 'I should be able to cope'

❏ 'why is everyone getting at me?'

❏ 'no one understands'

❏ 'I don't know what to do'

❏ 'I can't cope'

❏ 'what's the point?'

❏ 'I don't seem to be able to get on top of things'

❏ 'I keep forgetting where I put things'

❏ loss of judgement

Your stress rating

Add up your score to check how stressed you are.

0 – 4 symptoms: You are unlikely to be stressed.

5 – 8 symptoms: You are experiencing a mild form of stress and are not coping as well as you could. You need to make some changes to your life.

9 – 12 symptoms: You are experiencing a moderate degree of stress. You need to make major changes to your life.

13 or more symptoms: You need to take urgent action to reduce your stress levels. The higher your score, the more urgent is the need for action.

Stress is impossible to eliminate totally from life. Recognition of its symptoms and effects helps to reduce stress in your life so that you can avoid long-term damage to your health.

These Check Your Stress Level tables, symptoms list and test scores appear in the 4Health website in the Stress Gym section (http://www.channel4/health).

STRESS-LESS STRATEGIES

Before you can help students cope with their problems so that they can be ready to learn, you must take time to care of yourself. It is vitally important that you maintain a work-life balance to be effective as a teacher. Getting into healthy habits during your NQT year is a step towards a successful and enjoyable career.

Top tips

- Make a list of things that you enjoy doing that are good for you. Arrange to do one a day.
- Exercise. It can be difficult to fit this into a busy teaching schedule, but exercise is proven to elevate mood, improve health, wellbeing and body-image.
- Try to eat well. It is all too tempting to grab a soft drink or chocolate bar during the brief free times you have during the day. But eating healthily is an excellent way to maintain energy levels, therefore reducing stress. So reach for a piece of fruit instead of junk. Drink water throughout the day to stay hydrated.
- Make time, at least once a week, to do something you enjoy, or at least have a night off from marking and lesson planning.
- Write down how you see yourself a year, five years, or ten years from now. Share your ideas and goals with someone you trust.
- Write down at least five of your worries. Rank the list by importance in your life. By each worry write *Accept, Change,* or *Reject.* For each worry decide what your first step will be toward accepting, changing or rejecting it. Carry out the steps you listed.

cont./..

- Join in with social activities at your school.
- Use visualisations. Imagine a picture of a relaxing scene. You could even print it or cut it out from a magazine and put it on the front of your planner. Look at it when you feel stressed or need to put things in perspective.

"I always set aside some time in the evening where I can just sit and have a cup of tea or eat some dinner and switch my brain off. I know it sounds sad, but I watch Neighbours and Home and Away and that gives me a breather before I start doing any marking or lesson preparation that I need to do." Kerry J, Modern foreign languages teacher, London

DEATH BY TLA (THREE LETTER ABBREVIATION)

It may seem that nowhere in life can you escape the dreaded TLA and that everyone in power spends the majority of their time creating new and imaginative abbreviations. Teaching must be one of the worst serial offenders for this. Don't worry if you can't keep up; most experienced teachers can't either. Below are some of the most common and, hopefully, the easiest to remember.

PEOPLE

AST	Advanced Skills Teacher
EVC	Educational Visits Co-ordinator
EWO	Educational Welfare Officer
HoD	Head of Department
HoY	Head of Year
LSA	Learning Support Assistant
NQT	Newly Qualified Teacher
SENCO	Special Educational Needs Co-ordinator
SMG	Senior Management Group
SMT	Senior Management Team

QUALIFICATIONS/COURSES

ESOL	English as a Second or Other Language
GCSE: A level	General Certificate of Secondary Education, Advanced Level
GCSE: AS	General Certificate of Secondary Education, Advanced Supplementary examination
MFL	Modern Foreign Language
QTS	Qualified teacher status

MISCELLANEOUS

GTC	General Teaching Council
IAP	Individual Action Plan
IEP	Individual Education Plan
IIP	Investors in People
INSET	In-service education and training
LEA	Local Education Authority
MPS	Main Pay Scale
NC	National Curriculum
NLS	National Literacy Strategy
NNS	National Numeracy Strategy
RoA	Record of Achievement
SEN	Special Educational Needs
SOW	Schemes of work

KEY WORKER HOUSING

In this day and age you don't usually get anything for free. This rings true for most professions. However, if you are a teacher then there may be some help out there which you may not have considered.

Key worker housing is a system which has been implemented in much of the South-East and other areas suffering from a lack of key workers including teachers.

There may be help out there for you to get into affordable housing. Renting is one of the options open to teachers and many of the housing associations are running the key worker scheme. It will enable you to live on your salary.

One of the authors of this book began teaching in Essex after coming to train there. Although it took a little over a year on a waiting list, he and his wife were provided with a brand new top-floor two-bedroom apartment in a very nice, new city centre development. The rent was a lot less than expected. In fact, it was about a quarter of the standard rent for the area and it made a real difference.

How do you go about it? Your first port of call should be your council's local housing department. You can expect to wait for hours and fill in numerous forms, but it is the essential first stage. Get your name onto the waiting list and you are halfway there. The council will be able to provide you with a list of local housing associations. Your next step is to either contact them or the Citizen's Advice Bureau. Another step you can take is to talk to your school as they may have a more direct form of access than you have. After all the form filling and queuing, you have to wait for the cogs of bureaucracy to turn.

Eventually, you will be told if you are eligible. One small point: you are not given a great deal of choice or time to decide if you want what's offered. If you turn it down then, normally, that's it. So choose carefully.

Another system which is employed by some housing associations is the assisted mortgage. This simply means that they will provide a percentage of the cost of the mortgage, normally the deposit. You will then pay your mortgage and rent for the proportion of the money loaned to you by the housing association. This does mean that when you come to sell the house you must pay back the percentage borrowed and not the actual amount.

The best advice that we can give you is to talk to a financial professional, seek guidance from the Citizen's Advice Bureau and the county council and don't take "no" for an answer.

Top tips

- Go to the local housing officer in your local council and get your name down on as many waiting lists as possible. Take a pen and some proof of employment (check what you need before going). You will need to be really patient as the wait can be a long one.
- Seek advice from those qualified to give it. The best place to start is the Citizen's Advice Bureau, as they can offer full and impartial help. Again, this may involve waiting for some time and it's a good idea to ring for an appointment, rather than going straight to their offices.

WHY JOIN A UNION?

PROS AND CONS OF MEMBERSHIP

As an NQT you will have discounted or free membership of a union (depending on which one you join) so if it's parting with your precious cash that you're worried about, then there's no excuse. The three largest unions are the National Union of Teachers (NUT), National Association of Schoolmasters and Union of Women Teachers (NASUWT) and the Association of Teachers and Lecturers (ATL).

In today's litigious society you really need the help a union can give. If you ever have any problems, they can provide advice, support and legal help. It is highly advisable to join a union.

There's a great deal more to union activity than most people think; it is with these large organisations that governments negotiate the future of teaching in this country. The only real down-side to union membership is the annual subscription you have to pay. Most people pay monthly and it's usually about £10–15 a month after your first year, a small price to pay for peace of mind.

UNION REPRESENTATIVES

Most people won't ever talk to their school's union representative unless salaries are being discussed. The impending change of the pay structure has kept most union representatives very busy. They are a handy source of union information and can represent you in any disciplinary situations should you want them to.

A good union representative is the go-between for you when dealing with issues you are not comfortable with. They can act on your behalf and should always be there to support the union member. If the problem is complex, then your union representative will involve someone higher up in the union who will come to your school and act on your behalf.

MATERNITY AND PATERNITY RIGHTS

If you happen to become pregnant during your NQT year, don't worry. It's far more common than you'd think. Just remember that you normally have five years to complete a programme of induction.

GENERAL INFORMATION REGARDING MATERNITY RIGHTS

All employed pregnant women are entitled to 26 weeks of ordinary maternity leave, regardless of how long they have worked for their employer.

Those who have worked for their employer for 26 weeks continuously by the beginning of the 14th week before the baby is due can take 26 weeks of additional maternity leave. Additional maternity leave starts immediately after ordinary maternity leave and is usually unpaid.

Most women will get either Statutory Maternity Pay (SMP) from their employer or Maternity Allowance (MA) from the Department for Work and Pensions (DWP). Both are payable for up to 26 weeks and can be paid even if you have left work.

To get SMP you must have worked continuously for your employer into the 15th week before your baby is due and earn at least £77 a week on average. SMP is worth ninety per cent of your earnings for the first 6 weeks, followed by 20 weeks at £100 (or ninety per cent of your earnings for the full 26 weeks if this is less than £100).

To get SMP and leave from your employer, it is important to tell your employer that you are pregnant and when you want your maternity pay and leave to start. So check carefully on what you need to do.

TEACHERS' MATERNITY RIGHTS

Maternity, adoption and paternity pay are all dependent on the length of continuous service. For part-time teachers the length of continuous service required and the amount of leave available is the same as for full-time teachers, but the pay is pro rata.

If a teacher simply moves from full-time to part-time employment with the same employer without a break in employment, the accrued maternity rights she has move with her to the new job. Moves between sectors of education and breaks in employment have an effect on maternity rights. Statutory maternity leave and pay are as follows:

Maternity

26 weeks' unpaid leave with no service requirement.

26 weeks' statutory maternity pay if 26 weeks' continuous service by the qualifying week (15th week before expected week of childbirth). It is important to note that the rate of statutory maternity pay is based on your average weekly pay received during the eight weeks (two monthly salary payments) immediately before the qualifying week.

If you do not qualify for statutory maternity pay you may be entitled to 26 weeks' maternity allowance if you have worked for 26 weeks in the 66 weeks ending with the expected week of childbirth.

Paternity

Two weeks' paid leave if continuously employed for 26 weeks by the 15th week before the expected week of childbirth (statutory paternity pay).

Adoption

26 weeks' paid leave if 26 weeks' service by the date of matching (statutory adoption pay).

The Burgundy Book

The Burgundy Book gives full details of national conditions of service for school teachers in England and Wales, including the quite generous Burgundy Book maternity scheme for teachers on maternity leave, which is independent of Statutory Maternity Pay. It is important to note, however, that it you do take advantage of this scheme, you must return to work for three months full-time or six months part-time. Otherwise you will be required to repay the money (not all of it – three months' at half-pay, which, if you are not sure if you are going to return, can be deferred) to your local education authority.

Your school will have the Burgundy Book and it is usually the headteacher's secretary who is the best point of contact for enquiries into maternity leave.

Contact your union for further information and advice regarding your entitlements. If you defer your union membership while you are on maternity leave, make sure you return to full membership as soon as you return to work.

USEFUL WEBSITES

(All websites were operational in April 2006)

BEHAVIOUR

Behaviour UK. A free information portal covering behavioural issues
http://www.behaviouruk.com.

Behaviour4learning exists to promote excellence in services for children and young people who have emotional and behavioural difficulties and to support those who work with them.
http://www.behaviour4learning.ac.uk

Social, Emotional and Behavioural Difficulties Association (SEBDA). This consortium is made up of a number of partners. They work together to assist training providers in the work they do with trainees in the area of behaviour management.
http://www.sebda.org/

CURRICULUM

National Curriculum in Action uses pupils' work and case studies to exemplify the National Curriculum for England. This website is a searchable resource for school teachers and management which illustrates how the National Curriculum works in practice.
http://www.ncaction.org.uk

www.alcoholconcern.org.uk, the national agency on alcohol misuse.

www.drc-gb.org, the website for the Disability Rights Commission.

www.everychildmatters.gov.uk, website for a big project across England which involves everyone who works with children. This includes teachers, doctors, nurses, social workers, youth workers and many other people.

www.gtce.org.uk, the website of the General Teaching Council For England (GTCE)

www.gtcs.org.uk, the website of the General Teaching Council for Scotland (GTCS).

www.gtcw.org.uk, the website of the General Teaching Council for Wales (GTCW).

EMOTIONAL LITERACY

Antidote is a pioneering organisation that seeks to shape a more emotionally literate society through its work with schools. *http://www.antidote.org.uk/*

Sapere is an educational charity interested in the role of philosophical enquiry in education. The website is intended as a guide to philosophy for children in the UK. *http://sapere.org.uk/*

School of Emotional Literacy is an organisation which specialises in training professionals on how to use emotional literacy in the classroom, with details of some of the work

being done in this area in the UK and Europe today.
http://www.schoolofemotional-literacy.com

KEY WORKER HOUSING

Citizens' Advice Bureau
http://www.adviceguide.org.uk

Key Worker Living gives information about key worker living schemes.
http://www.keyworkerliving.co.uk

LOOKING AFTER YOURSELF

4Health, the Channel 4 website health portal.
http://www.channel4.com/health/

British Association for Counselling and Psychotherapy (BACP) is the UK's professional membership association for counsellors and psychotherapists
http://www.bacp.co.uk/

Centre for Stress Management offers stress management training and counselling programmes. Includes self-help material.
www.managingstress.com/

International Stress Management Association (ISMA) is the leading professional body for stress management. Their website has articles from their journal Stress News, links and general advice on lifestyle.
www.isma.org.uk/

The Stress Management Society. Here you can learn more about stress and its management.
www.stress.org.uk/

NEWS AND MEDIA

SecEd. The weekly newspaper for secondary education.
http://www.sec-ed.co.uk

Teachers' TV is an innovative digital TV channel to help teachers and schools to learn by sharing practical ideas and information.
http://www.teachers.tv

Times Educational Supplement (TES). This is the internet version of the Times Educational Supplement.
http://www.tes.co.uk

TEACHING UNIONS

Association of Teachers and Lecturers,
7 Northumberland Street,
London WC2N 5RD.
T: 020 7930 6441
F: 020 7930 1359
E: info@atl.org.uk
http://www.askatl.org.uk/

National Union of Teachers,
Hamilton House,
Mabledon Place,
London WC1H 9BD.
T: 020 7388 7230.
http://www.teachers.org.uk

National Association of School Masters
and Union of Women Teachers,
Hillscourt Education Centre,
Rose Hill,
Rednal,
Birmingham B45 8RS.
T: 0121 453 6150
F: 0121 457 6208/9
E: nasuwt@mail.nasuwt.org.uk
http://www.teachersunion.org.uk

TEACHING ASSISTANTS

The National Association of
Professional Teaching Assistants,
PO Box 210,
Cambridge CB4 3ZW.
T: 01223 224930
F: 01223 224934
E:info@napta.org.uk

BIBLIOGRAPHY

DfES (2002) *Special Educational Needs Code of Practice.* DfES Publications Centre, Annesley, Nottingham

DfES (2005) *Managing Medications in Schools and Early Years Settings.* DfES Publications Centre, Annesley, Nottingham

Drug and Alcohol Education and Prevention Team (2005) *Ritalin (Methylphenidate) in Schools – A Briefing Paper.* DrugScope and Alcohol Concern, London

Goleman D (1996) *Emotional Intelligence. Why it can matter more than IQ.* Bloomsbury, London

Local Government Employers (LGE) (2000) *Conditions of Service for School Teachers in England and Wales (The Burgundy Book).* LGE, London

NUT (1999) *Health & Safety Briefing: Tackling Stress.* NUT, London

The Special Educational Needs and Disability Act (2001) HMSO, London

The University of Bristol Graduate School of Education (2005) *The Bristol Guide.* Document Summary Service, Bristol

UNICEF (1991) *The Convention on the Rights of the Child.* The United Kingdom Committee for UNICEF, London

Vygotsky LS (1978) *Mind and society: The development of higher mental processes.* Harvard University Press, Cambridge, Ma

FURTHER READING

Cowley S (2002) *Getting the Buggers to Behave*. Continuum International Publishing Group, London

DfES (2003) *Every Child Matters Summary.* DfES Publications, Annesley, Nottingham

DfES (2005) *The Education (School Teachers' Pay and Conditions) Order 2005.* HMSO, London

Gardner H (1983) *Frames of Mind: the Theory of Multiple Intelligences.* Basic Books, NY

Sedgwick F (2005) *How to Teach with a Hangover.* Continuum International Publishing Group, London